SPIRIT-FILLED
JESUS

VLADIMIR SAVCHUK

ISBNs: 978-1-951201-00-5 (Print)

978-1-951201-03-6 (Ebook)

Contents

Introduction

Jesus, who was fully God and man, lived a sinless life here on earth. He modeled what a life surrendered to the Holy Spirit should be, so we can learn from Him what a living relationship with the Holy Spirit looks like.

Jesus depended on the Holy Spirit. He defended the Holy Spirit and His activity. Then at His ascension, He prayed to the Father that His followers would have the same power available to them. However, as modern believers, we have worked very hard to minimize our dependence on the Holy Spirit. Some have gone as far as to develop a new trinity: God the Father, God the Son, and the Holy Scriptures—pushing the Spirit of God out of the way and replacing Him with the book. The Holy Spirit wrote the Bible, but He is greater than the Bible, as usually the author is greater than the book.

Jesus is the Lamb of God.

> Behold! The Lamb of God who takes
> away the sin of the world! (John 1:29)

He is also the One who baptizes with the Holy Spirit.

> Upon whom you see the Spirit
> descending, and remaining on Him,

this is He who baptizes with the Holy
Spirit. (John 1:33)

> **Eternal life doesn't exist outside
> of Jesus Christ, and an abundant
> life doesn't exist outside of the
> Holy Spirit. Jesus came to give us
> both.**

As the Lamb of God, Jesus gives us eternal life; but as
the baptizer with the Holy Spirit, Jesus gives us abundant
life. Eternal life doesn't exist outside of Jesus Christ, and
an abundant life doesn't exist outside of the Holy Spirit.
Jesus came to give us both.

The thief does not come except to
steal, and to kill, and to destroy. I have
come that they may have life, and that
they may have it more abundantly.
(John 10:10)

Satan takes life, but Jesus gives life, and life more abundantly. The word for *life* in this context in Greek is *zoe*,
which is the very life that God has in Himself. Jesus gives
us that eternal life of God upon our salvation because He
gave His life as a lamb for us. But the Lord doesn't stop
there; He also offers us life abundantly. Abundant life is a
life overflowing with the Holy Spirit. No wonder John the
Baptist revealed that Jesus is both the Lamb of God and

and will be in you." All that time, as the disciples were with Jesus, they were actually with the Holy Spirit. It was the Holy Spirit who opened their eyes to Jesus as their promised Messiah. The Holy Spirit was with the disciples.

So now that the price for sin was paid for, and God's plan of redemption completed through the resurrection, Jesus breathed on His followers to give them the Holy Spirit.

> And when He had said this, He breathed
> on them, and said to them, "Receive the
> Holy Spirit." (John 20:22)

The Holy Spirit went from being *with* them to dwelling *in* them. He is with us to bring us to Christ, but He is in us to make us more like Christ.

But it didn't stop there. A few weeks later, as Jesus promised, the Holy Spirit came *upon* them, and they received power to fulfill His purpose.

> But you shall receive power when the
> Holy Spirit has come upon you; and you
> shall be witnesses to Me in Jerusalem,
> and in all Judea and Samaria, and to the
> end of the earth. (Acts 1:8)

The Holy Spirit coming upon us is what we call the baptism of the Holy Spirit. It's a powerful experience, and the purpose for it isn't tongues, but to release the power to evangelize. Bill Johnson, the pastor of Bethel Church

(Redding, California) likes to say, "He is in me for me; He is upon me for you."

The Holy Spirit is *with* us to bring us to *salvation*.

The Holy Spirit is *in* us to bring *sanctification*.

The Holy Spirit is *upon* us for *service*.

> **Supernatural life begins with a spiritual birth. Our relationship with the Holy Spirit starts when we get saved.**

Supernatural life begins with a spiritual birth. Our relationship with the Holy Spirit starts when we get saved.

following the Lord has made your situation very challenging financially. Fear not, the Holy Spirit brought you to this; He will bring you through it. Speak God's Word, praise His name, and remember His promises to you. Don't make this difficult time longer by giving in to your feelings instead of feeding yourself with God's truth. The Holy Spirit hides in the Holy Scriptures during the wilderness times.

Empowered By the Spirit

Then Jesus returned in the power of
the Spirit to Galilee, and news of Him
went out through all the surrounding
region. (Luke 4:14)

J esus was born by the Spirit, filled with the Spirit,
led by the Spirit, and sustained by the Spirit in the
wilderness by standing on the Holy Scriptures.
After passing the wilderness test, Jesus returned in the
power of the Spirit to minister healing and deliverance
to those in need.

The secret of Jesus' ministry was the Holy Spirit. The
source of miracles was the Holy Spirit. The power by
which He cast out demons, healed the sick, and raised
the dead was the Holy Spirit.

We call this power "the anointing." Jesus set an example
that ministry should be done with the anointing. Appoint-
ing needs anointing, and calling needs God's power.

Without the anointing, we treat the calling as a career or a
job instead of ministry.

Ministry is different from a career. A career requires a diploma; a calling requires anointing. A career is natural; a calling is supernatural. A career changes; a calling doesn't. This doesn't mean that education and schooling are not needed for ministry. But college can't give an anointing, the Holy Spirit gives that. We can't do the spiritual aspects of our ministry with degrees. Demons don't get cast out because of our education. People don't get healed because we have information. These things are important, but Jesus' ministry was marked by the power of the Holy Spirit. Ours should be too.

After Jesus returned in the power of the Holy Spirit, demons started to get cast out, sicknesses were healed, the gospel of the kingdom was proclaimed, and disciples were made. In other words, the ministry started. There wasn't a building, paid staff, social media pages, marketing, or church programs—just ministry empowered by the Spirit. Today, we focus ministry more on programs, staff, marketing, budget, and buildings. Jesus started His ministry with the Holy Spirit.

> But you shall receive power when the
> Holy Spirit has come upon you; and you
> shall be witnesses to Me in Jerusalem,
> and in all Judea and Samaria, and to the
> end of the earth. (Acts 1:8)

Jesus promised the same to us, that we will receive power when the Spirit comes upon us. The power of the Holy Spirit is not for us, but for others. It's not for status, but for service. This power is not meant to validate a person, but to glorify Jesus. This power is not even for miracles, but to draw people to salvation. Healing, deliverance, and all of God's blessings are meant to reveal Jesus, point to the cross, and draw men to eternal salvation. The greatest miracle is the salvation of a soul. As Jesus came to seek and save that which was lost, the power of the Holy Spirit was there to help accomplish that mission. It is the same with us—His power is not to make us famous or rich or even powerful, but to help us serve people and bring as many as possible to salvation.

Miracles are the best method of evangelism. Miracles are what the Holy Spirit does. We see more and more people come to Jesus after they experience Jesus. Through the Holy Spirit, we can explain Jesus, but people can also experience Him. *"Oh, taste and see that the Lord is good"* (Psalm 34:8).

Recently, a couple came to church who were both healed physically. The husband had an ankle issue, and the wife had pain in the hips. After worship, we prayed for healing, and they both felt the pain was gone. That service they got saved. Some time has passed since then, and they still have no pain! I see them at church, filled with new life and bringing others to church. That's the purpose of miracles—to draw men to Christ. Jesus and the early church didn't have a non-profit status or a marketing strategy to reach their community. Their strategy was the Holy Spirit. Miracles did all the marketing.

> **Jesus and the early church didn't have a non-profit status or a marketing strategy to reach their community. Their strategy was the Holy Spirit.**

Francis Chan mentioned a story in one of his sermons of a Chinese pastor who leads an underground church in Shanghai. This pastor told Francis that the Chinese church has five pillars that make it successful in the midst of persecution. These five pillars are as follows:

1. They are devoted to the Word of God.

2. They are deeply devoted to prayer.

3. They expect every believer to share the gospel.

4. They expect miracles to happen regularly.

5. They embrace suffering for Jesus.

The Holy Spirit is moving powerfully in persecuted parts of the world because believers depend more on His power and less on our human methods. Most of the activities in the church today wouldn't stop if the Spirit of God would be removed. Sadly, we are in danger of falling into the backslidden state, as people on the last day were described by Paul: *"Having a form of godliness but denying its power"* (2 Timothy 3:5).

As we advance in technology and knowledge, we must remember the world is more spiritual than we realize. We are in a spiritual war that can only be won by spiritual weapons. The words of prophet Zechariah remind us that it's " *'Not by might nor by power, but by My Spirit,' Says the Lord of hosts. 'Who are you, O great mountain? Before Zerubbabel you shall become a plain! And he shall bring forth the capstone with shouts of 'Grace, grace to it! ' "* (Zechariah 4:6-7). If we want to level mountains of opposition and birth forth capstones on the temple of our God, it will be by His Spirit, not our might.

Every Sunday we have a team that goes on the street to pray for the sick and then tell them of the good news of Jesus' love. We see many healings and people respond to the message when they experience the gospel. One of the ways people experience Jesus is by receiving His goodness and mercy in a tangible way.

Not only do we need the Spirit's anointing to pray for the sick and to cast out demons, but to preach the gospel.

> "The Spirit of the Lord is upon Me,
> because He has anointed Me to preach
> the gospel to the poor. (Luke 4:18)

Jesus was anointed to preach. Without the anointing of the Holy Spirit, preaching is nothing more than a motivational speech. When I share with younger preachers about preaching, I try to contrast anointed preaching and motivational speaking. I am not against motivational speakers, but the church pulpit is not a stage for speaking about self-help ideas, but to exalt Jesus. Motivational speaking is man-centered. Anointed preaching is Christ-centered. Motivational speaking is usually light, fun, humorous, and entertaining. Anointed preaching produces a holy hunger for God and respect for His Word.

> **Without the anointing of the Holy Spirit, preaching is nothing more than a motivational speech.**

When God's anointing is on your speaking, you become like salt. When people taste salt, they become thirsty for water. When people come in contact with anointed preaching, it produces a hunger for God and His Word. Motivational speaking that's void of the Holy Spirit is like sugar. Sugar is sweet and addictive. When you eat sugar, you want more sugar. When you listen to just motivational, fun, entertaining speeches, you want more of the speaker, not more of Jesus. It's sugar, not salt. It's sweet, but too much of it is dangerous to your spiritual health if it doesn't produce a hunger for Jesus in you. Like Oswald Chambers said, "Anything that flatters me in my preaching of the gospel will result in making me a traitor to Jesus, and I prevent the creative power of His redemption from doing its work."

> **To walk in the anointing, we must walk in the Holy Spirit.**

To walk in the anointing, we must walk in the Holy Spirit. If we are living in the flesh and feeding our sinful mind, our life and ministry will not be saturated with God's grace, but only with human strength and wisdom.

Offered Himself as a Sacrifice

How much more shall the blood of Christ,
who through the eternal Spirit offered
Himself without spot to God, cleanse
your conscience from dead works to serve
the living God? (Hebrews 9:14-15)

Jesus modeled a Spirit-filled life. He was born by the Spirit, filled by the Spirit, led by the Spirit, and empowered by the Spirit. But it didn't end there. The Holy Spirit helped Jesus to offer Himself as a sacrifice for the sins of the world. The Holy Spirit helped Jesus to endure suffering because of His yes to the Father. He is able to help us endure the sufferings we face as a result of following the will of God.

The question of suffering has plagued skeptics and theologians as long as suffering has existed. Even though suffering is not a popular topic these days, Scripture has much to say about it. The Bible deals more with the *how* of suffering than the *why* of suffering. It teaches us more about how we should suffer instead of why we are suffering.

These things I have spoken to you,
that in Me you may have peace. In the
world you will have tribulation; but
be of good cheer, I have overcome the
world. (John 16:33)

That's the promise of Jesus: in this world you will have suffering—but Jesus doesn't end there. He inspires courage in believers to suffer with joy, because Jesus is our ultimate Victor, and the Holy Spirit is our Helper. Having joy in our suffering comes as a shock to us because our culture is built on pursuing happiness. Peter said, "*But rejoice to the extent that you partake of Christ's sufferings, that when His glory is revealed, you may also be glad with exceeding joy*" (1 Peter 4:13). It's impossible to be happy while suffering, but rejoicing in suffering is possible. Joy is based on the presence of the Holy Spirit, while happiness is an emotion based on what's happening to us.

> **Joy is based on the presence of the Holy Spirit, while happiness is an emotion based on what's happening to us.**

Some view the Holy Spirit as Someone who can take away all our suffering because He is the Source of miracles, healings, and deliverance. The closer we get to the Holy Spirit, the further we will be from suffering. But that view is flawed. Jesus, who was fully God but also fully man and filled with the Holy Spirit, endured extreme suffering. But He didn't go through this pain and rejection alone; He had the help of the Holy Spirit.

Every suffering is not created equal. Jesus was suffering on the cross, but He wasn't the only one there. There were two other criminals suffering there as well for their sins. One of those sinners repented; the other didn't. While we all experience general suffering because of the sin in the world, some of us experience intense suffering because of our personal sin. Others experience intense suffering because of our surrender to the will of God.

Jesus was on the cross due to His obedience to the Father; the thieves were there due to their disobedience—the same situation for different reasons—the same situation, but with different outcomes. Jesus rose from the dead; those next to him on the cross didn't. Our YES to God can put us on the cross. In fact, *"Then Jesus said to His disciples, "If anyone desires to come after Me, let him deny himself, and take up his cross, and follow Me"* (Matthew 16:24). Living in the obedience of the Lord landed Joseph in prison. Refusing to bow to an idol put Shadrach, Meshach, and Abednego into the furnace of fire. Preaching the gospel and healing the sick man got the apostles physically beaten. Delivering a demon-possessed girl in Phillipi got Paul beaten and jailed. Persecution, poverty, false accusation, and attack from every side can be the portion of those who choose God's will. There are sufferings that God delivers us from, but there are those who follow our obedience to Him that His

43

Spirit helps us through. *You therefore must endure hardship as a good soldier of Jesus Christ* (2 Timothy 2:3).

When was the last time you suffered because of your surrender to God? Too many people suffer because of a lack of surrender to God.

> For what credit is it if, when you are
> beaten for your faults, you take it
> patiently? But when you do good and
> suffer, if you take it patiently, this is
> commendable before God. For to this you
> were called, because Christ also suffered
> for us, leaving us an example, that you
> should follow His steps. (1 Peter 2:20-21)

Those who want to please God must be more addicted to the Comforter than they are attached to their comforts.

The Holy Spirit is called our Comforter. We truly discover the Comforter when we go through rejection, persecution, attacks, suffering, and even poverty for the sake of the gospel. Those who want to please God must be more addicted to the Comforter than they are attached to their comforts. The world seeks to make their life as comfortable as possible; the Bible teaches us to stay as close to the Comforter as we can. A life of following God's call will take us through valleys, prisons, dry pits, fiery furnaces, storms, shipwrecks, and crosses. We should not seek suffering but surrender to God's will. Carrying the cross is not inflicting pain on yourself. It's living with this motto: *"Not my will, but Yours, be done"* (Luke 22:42). Putting God's will before our will is what carrying the cross means. Dying to our self-interests, ego, and pride will result in sacrifice.

While everyone will most likely suffer while on this earth, we have the privilege of suffering because of our surrender to God's will. When we do that, we will not be carrying the cross alone:

- The Holy Spirit will walk with us through the valley so we don't fear evil.

- He will be with us in the furnace of fire so we don't get burned.

- The Comforter will stay with us in the storm so we don't drown.

- He will even go with us to prison to bring peace into our hearts.

- If the world rejects us, He will quiet us with His love.

- If our family and friends forsake us, He will always be near.

- If the cross becomes too heavy, He will give us strength.

I used to be afraid of making sacrifices due to the suffering that it would bring. But after discovering the person of the Holy Spirit and how He helped Jesus through the cross, I am more relaxed knowing that I am yoked with the Holy

Spirit. My pain and struggle that comes from following God is shared with the Comforter. I can have His comfort if physical comforts are no longer accessible. All I have to do is surrender to Him in suffering. Wait on His presence while in pain. It's not only His presence that comforts us, but He also knows how to send the right person, sermon, book, or song that will bring comfort to us in our temporary affliction. *"Nevertheless God, who comforts the downcast, comforted us by the coming of Titus"* (2 Corinthians 7:6).

> But if the Spirit of Him who raised
> Jesus from the dead dwells in you, He
> who raised Christ from the dead will
> also give life to your mortal bodies
> through His Spirit who dwells in you.
> (Romans 8:11)

The Holy Spirit who helped Jesus get through the cross also raised Him from the dead. This is encouraging, not just because we can endure our spiritual crosses with the Comforter, but also knowing He will bring us through to the other side. He who raised Jesus from the dead dwells in us. He is able to do the same for us by bringing spiritual revival, a mighty renewal that will follow the cross-seasons of our life. Crucifixion led to the resurrection. When we walk with the Holy Spirit through the garden of Gethsemane where our will takes second place to God's will, He will bring us to the resurrection. That shouldn't come as a surprise; Jesus said, *"For whoever desires to save his life will lose it, but whoever loses his life for My sake will find it"* (Matthew 16:25).

Who helps us find this life? The same Holy Spirit who is with us to help us lose it! He dwells in us and wants to bring a spiritual revival, but this revival can't come until the Holy Spirit takes us through surrendering our will.

There's only three things someone can do with their life: wreck it by living sinfully, waste it by living selfishly, or awaken it by living in surrender to the will of God. Surrendering to the will of God is more than just praying the sinner's prayer—it's giving up selfish ways. That, my friend, is what the cross is all about. When we become believers, we come to the cross and see Jesus. When we become disciples, we get on the cross and see the dying world. When we become followers, we pick up that cross and live for God's will on this earth. The most amazing part about this journey is our friend, the Holy Spirit, who becomes our Comforter in the process. He leads us through suffering to sanctification; from the cross to resurrection; from death to self to new life in God. Many wish to have a revival but don't want to die to their will. Many wish to know the Holy Spirit as their Comforter but cling to their comforts. Many wish to have a resurrection but keep running from the cross.

If the Holy Spirit helped Jesus through the cross, He will help you. If He raised Jesus, He will raise you to a new level in life.

Conclusion

Jesus was born by the Spirit, filled by the Spirit, led by the Spirit, empowered by the Spirit, and offered Himself as a sacrifice on the cross by the eternal Spirit. He breathed the Holy Spirit on His disciples and prayed for the Father to send the Spirit to His followers.

Jesus modeled a life full of the Spirit, and He introduces us to the same life by giving us the Holy Spirit. When we are baptized into the Holy Spirit, guess who is doing that baptism? It's none other than Jesus, the Baptizer of the Holy Spirit. Many have met Jesus as a Lamb; now it's time to meet the Baptizer. Some have come to the cross, but now it's time to come to Pentecost.

Let Jesus' life be an example for us to follow—we are called to pick up our cross and follow Him. We can't do that unless we rely on the Holy Spirit the same way He did.

Other Books:

Break Free
Single, Ready to Mingle
Fight Back

Ebooks:

Walking in the Holy Spirit
From Secret Sin to Secret Place
FAQs about Deliverance
Seven Signs of Walking in the Holy Spirit

VladSchool

Then He said to His disciples, "The
harvest truly is plentiful, but the laborers are few. Therefore pray the Lord
of the harvest to send out laborers into
His harvest" (Matthew 9:37-38).

In 2020, we launched an online school to impact the world
by training up the laborers for God's harvest field. Many
believers around the world don't have the time to go to Bible
school or can't afford Bible training. Therefore, we make our
online school totally free.

Vlad's school consists of courses that are Spirit-filled,
practical, and scriptural about powerful topics such as deliverance, the Holy Spirit, prayer, ministry, identity in Christ, etc. All
of our classes are offered for free, thanks to the generous support
of our partners.

Available courses:
- Curses
- Foundations
- Anointing
- Dating without Fornicating
- Relationship with the Holy Spirit
- Deliverance from Demons
- And many more

Enroll today at www.vladschool.com to grow in the
Lord and to be trained in ministry.

About the Author

Vladimir Savchuk is a rising spiritual voice who God is using to profoundly impact this generation. Leveraging modern media technology to propagate the timeless truth of the faith, Pastor Vlad has written books, hosted conferences, and created content platforms that are touching hundreds and thousands of people all around the world.

Pastor Vlad's creative approach in leading Hungry Generation church has been used by the Holy Spirit to cultivate an anointed internship program and a worship culture with worldwide reach. He is a gifted speaker with an emphasis on rarely-addressed spiritual topics, such as spiritual warfare, deliverance, and the Holy Spirit. Pastor Vlad is declaring ancient truths in a modern way.

Vlad is married to his beautiful wife, Lana, with whom he enjoys spending time and doing ministry together.

Stay Connected

Facebook.com/vladhungrygen

Twitter.com/vladhungrygen

Instagram.com/vladhungrygen

YouTube.com/vladimirsavchuk

www.pastorvlad.org

www.vladschool.com

If you have a testimony from reading this e-book,
please email hello@pastorvlad.org

If you wish to post about this e-book on your social media,
please use tag @vladhungrygen and use #pastorvlad hashtag.

If you are looking for a video study guide for small groups,
you can find it at www.pastorvlad.org

Made in the USA
Las Vegas, NV
26 April 2024

89164161R00036